WHALES SET I

BELUGA WHALES

Megan M. Gunderson
ABDO Publishing Company

visit us at
www.abdopublishing.com

Published by ABDO Publishing Company, 8000 West 78th Street, Edina, Minnesota 55439.
Copyright © 2011 by Abdo Consulting Group, Inc. International copyrights reserved in all
countries. No part of this book may be reproduced in any form without written permission
from the publisher. The Checkerboard Library™ is a trademark and logo of ABDO
Publishing Company.

Printed in the United States of America, North Mankato, Minnesota.
042010
092010

Cover Photo: Alamy
Interior Photos: AP Images p. 15; © Brenna Hernandez / SeaPics.com p. 17;
   © John K.B. Ford / SeaPics.com p. 13; National Geographic Stock pp. 8, 21;
   Peter Arnold pp. 10, 19; Photo Researchers p. 14; Photolibrary p. 5;
   Uko Gorter pp. 7, 9

Editor: BreAnn Rumsch
Art Direction & Cover Design: Neil Klinepier

Library of Congress Cataloging-in-Publication Data

Gunderson, Megan M., 1981-
  Beluga whales / Megan M. Gunderson.
     p. cm. -- (Whales)
  Includes index.
  ISBN 978-1-61613-446-4
  1. White whale--Juvenile literature. I. Title.
  QL737.C433G86 2011
  599.5'42--dc22
              2010005540

CONTENTS

BELUGA WHALES AND FAMILY

Bright white beluga whales are popular with whale watchers and aquarium visitors. Like all mammals, belugas are **warm-blooded** and nurse their young. These **cetaceans** must surface to take deep breaths above water.

Beluga whales belong to the family Monodontidae. The only other member of their family is the narwhal. Both species live in the cold waters of the Arctic Ocean.

Beluga whales are noisy ocean dwellers. Their loud chirps and whistles can even be heard above water! This earned them the nickname sea canaries. Belugas are also called white whales. In fact, the name *beluga* comes from a Russian word meaning "white."

Belugas can imitate a variety of sounds.

SHAPE, SIZE, AND COLOR

A thick layer of **blubber** covers the beluga whale's broad, rounded body. The beluga's small, broad flippers sometimes curl up at the ends. The flukes have a deep notch in the center. Instead of a dorsal fin, there is a narrow dorsal ridge.

The beluga appears to have different facial expressions. This is because it can change the shape of its bulging **melon**. The neck is **flexible**, too. So, the beluga can turn its small head from side to side. And, it can nod up and down.

On average, male beluga whales grow 11 to 15 feet (3.4 to 4.6 m) long. They weigh about 3,300 pounds (1,500 kg). Females are smaller.

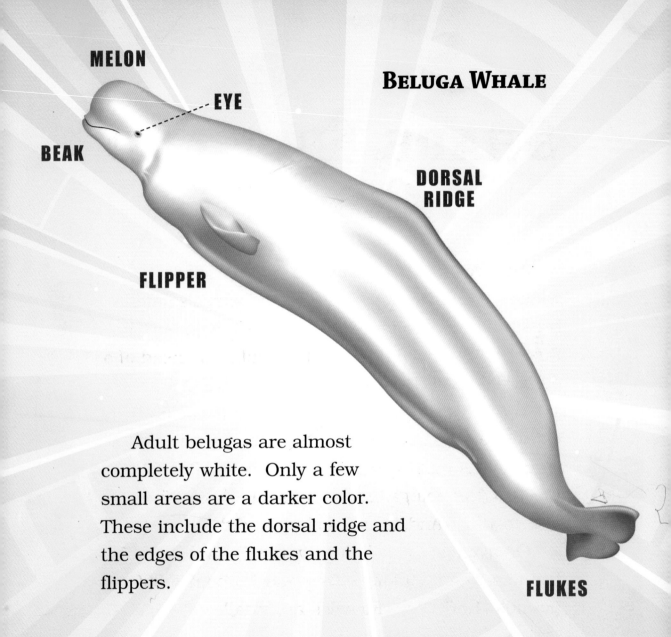

MELON

EYE

BEAK

BELUGA WHALE

DORSAL
RIDGE

FLIPPER

Adult belugas are almost
completely white. Only a few
small areas are a darker color.
These include the dorsal ridge and
the edges of the flukes and the
flippers.

FLUKES

7

WHERE THEY LIVE

Belugas live in the Arctic Ocean and its nearby seas, bays, and rivers. They are comfortable in freshwater and saltwater **habitats**. Belugas swim in both shallow and deep water.

In summer, belugas enter bays, **estuaries**, and rivers. There, they find food and raise their young. In autumn, they move because these areas freeze over. Some populations **migrate** longer distances than others.

In their habitat, beluga whales swim among huge ice formations.

Thousands of belugas may migrate together.

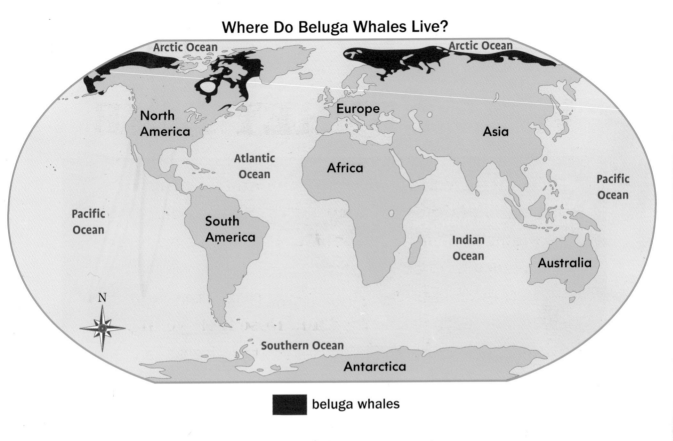

Where Do Beluga Whales Live?

beluga whales

Without dorsal fins, they glide easily under ice. Under thin ice, belugas can break open breathing holes using the **melon**. Yet they cannot break through thick ice. So, belugas must be careful not to get trapped!

SENSES

Underwater, a beluga's strong flukes work hard to push it up to spyhop!

Beluga whales are curious creatures. They use their excellent senses to explore their **habitat**. Belugas have good eyesight. To see above the surface, they bob their heads out of the water. This is called spyhopping.

Scientists believe belugas use their sense of taste. They do not think belugas have a sense of smell. But, scientists know touch is an important sense for belugas. Touching is one way belugas communicate with one another.

Most of all, belugas rely on hearing. This sense is useful in a **habitat** that is often dark and ice covered. Hearing is a vital part of a special ability called echolocation. Belugas use it to locate breathing holes, find prey, and avoid predators.

To use echolocation, a beluga makes a series of clicks. These sounds pass through the large **melon** and out into the water. They hit objects in the beluga's path. The sounds bounce back as echoes, which the beluga hears and understands. The echoes reveal an object's size, distance, and speed.

DEFENSE

Polar bears, killer whales, and humans are all beluga whale predators. Belugas trapped by ice can become polar bear prey. With one swipe of its paw, a bear can drag a beluga onto the ice for a meal!

A great sense of hearing helps belugas avoid killer whales. Like other **cetaceans**, killer whales make whistles and calls. If belugas hear killer whales approaching, they head for safety.

Belugas can try to escape danger. Normally, they swim 2 to 6 miles per hour (3 to 9 km/h). If they are being chased, belugas can swim 14 miles per hour (22 km/h). Unfortunately, swimming away from danger sometimes leads to **strandings**. Without help from humans, this can lead to death.

Pollution also causes **strandings**. This is just one threat belugas face from humans. People have been hunting them for hundreds of years. Today, the number of belugas that can be hunted is limited. Still, some populations remain threatened.

If belugas become trapped by ice, they are vulnerable to polar bears. They may also starve or drown.

FOOD

A beluga eats 50 to 60 pounds (23 to 27 kg) of food each day.

Like all **cetaceans**, belugas are carnivores. They eat shrimps, crabs, squid, octopuses, and marine worms. They also feast on salmon, arctic cod, herring, capelins, and other fish.

Belugas hunt these creatures in freshwater and salt water. To find their food, they dive down 65 to 1,150 feet (20 to 350 m). For each dive, they spend 9 to 13 minutes underwater.

On average, belugas have 32 to 36 teeth.

Belugas hunt along the bottom of their **habitat**. They squirt water into the ground to reveal hidden prey. Then, they pucker their lips to suck up their catch. To hunt schools of fish, belugas work together. They catch prey in their peglike teeth and swallow it whole!

BABIES

Beluga whales usually mate between late February and May. After mating, females may become **pregnant**. They carry their young for 12 to nearly 15 months.

A mother beluga almost always gives birth to one baby at a time. The baby is called a calf. Mothers deliver their calves in bays and **estuaries**.

A newborn beluga is about five feet (1.5 m) long. It weighs around 175 pounds (80 kg). A beluga calf is dark or bluish gray to brownish red in color. As it grows older, its color lightens. It will take seven to nine years to turn white.

Beluga calves need their mothers for food and safety. Calves nurse for at least 24 months. They learn much about survival from the adults around them. Beluga whales can live for more than 50 years.

Beluga calves can swim at birth.

BEHAVIORS

Beluga whales are very social animals. They form permanent **pods**. Often, group members are the same age and sex. Belugas also form nursery groups. These contain mothers and calves.

For **migrating** and feeding, pods may gather together to form much larger groups. Scientists have seen schools of 10,000 belugas!

Belugas have several special features that set them apart from other whales. They can swim backward. And, belugas **molt** every summer! The outer layer of skin turns yellow in winter. In summer, belugas rub along river bottoms to remove that outer layer.

Beluga whales are playful, curious creatures. In fact, they often approach boats. These bright white animals continue to fascinate whale watchers!

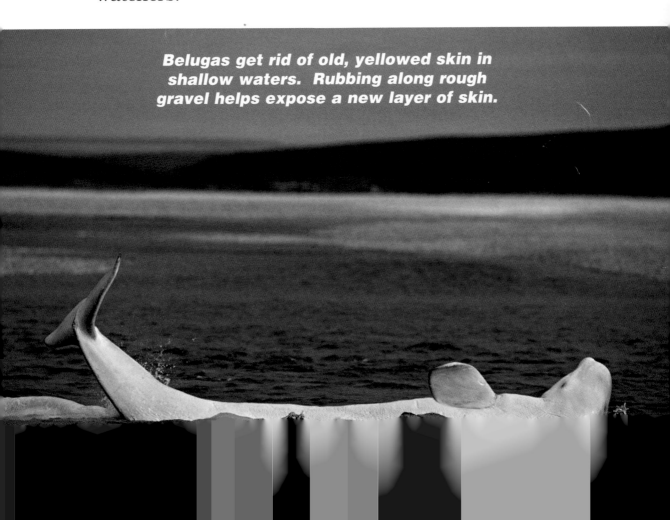

Belugas get rid of old, yellowed skin in shallow waters. Rubbing along rough gravel helps expose a new layer of skin.

BELUGA WHALE FACTS

Scientific Name: *Delphinapterus leucas*

Common Name: Beluga whale

Other Names: White whale, sea canary

Average Size:
Length - 11 to 15 feet (3.4 to 4.6 m) for males
Weight - 3,300 pounds (1,500 kg) for males
Females are smaller.

Where They Are Found: In the Arctic Ocean and its nearby seas, bays, and rivers

Beluga whales at a Japanese aquarium learned to blow bubbles for visitors!

GLOSSARY

blubber - the fat of whales and other marine mammals. Blubber protects animals from cold.

cetacean (sih-TAY-shuhn) - a member of the order Cetacea. Mammals such as dolphins, whales, and porpoises are cetaceans.

estuary (EHS-chuh-wehr-ee) - the area of water where a river's current meets an ocean's tide.

flexible - able to bend or move easily.

habitat - a place where a living thing is naturally found.

melon - a rounded structure found in the forehead of some cetaceans.

migrate - to move from one place to another, often to find food.

molt - to shed skin, hair, or feathers and replace with new growth.

pod - a group of socially connected dolphins or whales.

pregnant - having one or more babies growing within the body.

stranding - the appearance of a cetacean on a beach.

warm-blooded - having a body temperature that is not much affected by surrounding air or water.

WEB SITES

To learn more about beluga whales, visit ABDO Publishing Company on the World Wide Web at **www.abdopublishing.com**. Web sites about beluga whales are featured on our Book Links page. These links are routinely monitored and updated to provide the most current information available.

INDEX